# SNAP AND SHARE:

## EXPLORING THE POTENTIAL OF INSTAGRAM AND OTHER PHOTO AND VIDEO APPS

ADAM FURGANG

rosen publishing's
**rosen central**

New York

*For my best friend, Jesse Feigelman, who took great pictures and made great films*

Published in 2015 by The Rosen Publishing Group, Inc.
29 East 21st Street, New York, NY 10010

First Edition

**Library of Congress Cataloging-in-Publication Data**

Furgang, Adam, author.
Snap and share: exploring the potential of Instagram and other photo and video apps/Adam Furgang.—First edition.
    pages cm.—(Digital and information literacy)
Audience: Grades 5 to 8.
ISBN 978-1-4777-7934-7 (library bound)—ISBN 978-1-4777-7935-4 (pbk.)—ISBN 978-1-4777-7936-1 (6-pack)
1. Instagram (Firm)—Juvenile literature. 2. Photography—Digital techniques—Juvenile literature. 3. Image files—Juvenile literature. I. Title. II. Series: Digital and information literacy.
TR267.5.I57F87 2015
770.28553—dc23

2014010032

Manufactured in Malaysia

# CONTENTS

# INTRODUCTION

They say a picture is worth a thousand words. If that's true, then what are a thousand pictures worth? Today, with the use of smartphones, tablets, and similar devices containing miniaturized cameras, snapping and sharing photos has never been easier—or more commonplace.

It seems that the whole world is obsessed with taking pictures. It is estimated that as many as 880,000,000,000—almost 1 trillion!—photos will have been taken this year. That staggering number is due to the popularity of photo- and video-sharing applications for mobile devices.

In 2013, "selfie" was chosen as the Word of the Year by Oxford Dictionaries. They define a selfie as "a photograph that one has taken of oneself, typically one taken with a smartphone or webcam and uploaded to a social media website." The use of the word "selfie" rose over 17,000 percent in just that year alone. Even President Barack Obama and dozens of celebrities have been seen taking selfies with smartphones.

Before there were smartphones with cameras, the fastest way to take a photo of oneself and share it quickly was with a Polaroid camera. The print would come directly out of the camera and be visible to the viewer within a few minutes. Everyone from grandparents around the dinner table to pop artists such

President Barack Obama poses for a selfie with British Prime Minister David Cameron *(left)* and Denmark's Prime Minister, Helle Thorning-Schmidt.

as Andy Warhol were making use of the quick results of the Polaroid. Artists of the 1960s and 1970s helped contribute to the camera's popularity.

But the world changed with the introduction of cell phone cameras and social networking websites on the Internet. By 2009, digital photography, mobile phone camera technologies, and social networking had become so popular that Polaroid stopped manufacturing instant cameras as well as film. But the artsy technology of the 1970s was not forgotten. One of today's most popular photo-sharing apps, Instagram, has an icon that looks like an old Polaroid camera.

Using photo and video applications for mobile devices can be a lot of fun, and sharing your work with friends and family over social networking

Before mobile phone photography, the Polaroid camera allowed users to create prints within moments after taking the picture.

sites can make the experience even more exciting. To get started, you'll need a device such as a smartphone, iPod Touch, or tablet computer to take the photos. Then you'll need Wi-Fi or another Internet connection to send the digital images to social networking sites. In addition to staying in touch with friends and family, you can also use photo and video apps to explore your creative potential and even to do school assignments and presentations. Today, we have so many digital tools at our fingertips that it's easy to get your creative juices flowing.

# Chapter 1

# Instagram: Photos in an Instant

n only a few short years, the popularity of photo-sharing apps has exploded. Much of that popularity is due in part to the mobile app Instagram. The company was started in 2010 and has since grown in popularity at lightning speed. By 2012, the app had become so popular that the online social network Facebook negotiated to purchase the tiny start-up. By the time the deal was over, Instagram was purchased for $300 million and $12 million in stock. Today, even the White House has an official Instagram account, used for posting quick shots of life around the nation's most famous home office.

So what exactly is Instagram? Instagram is a photo-sharing app that allows users to take and share pictures and videos on its network; post to other online social networks such as Facebook, Twitter, Tumblr, and Flickr and send photos and videos to friends and family on their mobile phones. Photos taken with Instagram often have an antique, or retro, look and feel. The pictures are square, not the more typical rectangular format. Once an Instagram photo is taken with a mobile device, users can apply various

Today, mobile apps such as Instagram allow people to share a variety of images from all over the world.

virtual filters and frames to the image. The variety of results allows users to produce unique and artistic-looking photos.

Before jumping into the world of Instagram, there are a few things to know about setting up and using your account. Many of these steps apply to setting up accounts with other mobile apps as well.

File    Edit    View    Favorites    Tools    Help

INSTAGRAM DIRECT

## INSTAGRAM DIRECT

Instagram Direct is a feature that allows Instagram users to take a photo or video and share it directly with a single Instagram user. Photos or videos shared this way will only be visible to the recipient of your choice. The photos do not appear in one's feed, but need to be accessed separately in your inbox. A small icon will appear to alert you if someone has shared content with you this way. Use this feature when you want to share something with just one friend. This feature is perfect for inside jokes, private moments, or something only one special person will appreciate.

## Making Your Profile

Before you can get started taking and sharing Instagram pictures, you will need to download the app onto your mobile device. The app is free and can be downloaded from one of several online app stores, depending on the mobile device you use.

Once you have the Instagram app on your phone, you can launch, or open, it. From here, you will be asked to register with Instagram. You cannot use Instagram without first registering a unique username and password. Your username gives you a completely unique identity so that other friends using Instagram can easily find you. Be sure to keep your password a secret, though, so that only you and your parents can access your account.

Once the app is installed, look at the bottom of your screen. There, you will see five icons, or tabs. From left to right, the tabs are: Home,

The Explore tab on the Instagram app allows the user to see a random selection of public images posted by other Instagram users.

Explore, Camera, News Feed, and Profile. Each one of these button tabs will help you quickly navigate the app to exactly where you want to go.

When you are ready to start using the app, you can update your profile, start taking pictures, or find other friends using Instagram to follow. To find other "Instagramers," go to your profile. From there, click Find Friends if you're on an Android device or Find and Invite Friends if you are on an iPhone. Friends can be found from either Facebook or your list of contacts already on your phone. The Instagram app may ask for permission to access your contacts. This is OK and is just a safety feature so that you are aware of what the app is doing.

## Privacy Settings

Before you snap and share your first picture, it's a good

idea to familiarize yourself with Instagram's privacy settings. Take some extra time here so that you can use the app safely and responsibly.

Aside from just taking photos and videos and sharing them, you will also be able to see the photos that friends have taken and shared with you. The photos and videos taken by others that you are connected with can be seen on your feed.

You can choose to follow only people you know, or you can explore photos shared publicly by other Instagram users. Some celebrities share their Instagram photos publicly and have a huge list of followers. Use caution and adult guidance before following anyone whom you do not know personally.

You can also set your profile so that your posts are hidden from the public and only friends and family you approve can see what you share. Setting up your Instagram profile this way is a good idea. For more detailed help with Instagram, visit the website's Help section.

## Your Feed

Whenever you open Instagram, you will see the most recent photo that one of your contacts has shared. You can scroll down to see older pictures in your feed. When you see a picture you like, you can click the Like tab to show the user and all his or her followers that you like that photo. You can also comment on a photo by clicking the Comment button. Once you click the Comment button, a text field will appear, as well as your phone's keypad. Type your comment and then click the Send button to post the comment. Remember to be respectful and mature with your comments.

## Taking Pictures & Video

Now it's time to take your first picture! Find the camera tab at the bottom of the screen and click on it to activate your camera. Once you have framed the person or object you want to take a picture of, hold your phone steady, and touch and release the button at the bottom of your screen. If you hold the button down, you will be able to continue framing your picture, and the shot will be taken when you remove your finger.

Once the picture has been taken, you will see it on the phone's screen. From here, you have some choices for editing and adding filters. Scroll through the filters to see how they will adjust the photo you just took. Vintage colors, black and white, and warm and cool variations are all available. Experiment with these until you find one you like. After this, add frames and play with the few other available adjustments, such as making the picture lighter or darker or adding selective focus to a particular area. Many of these features mimic qualities often found in professional cameras or more complex photo-editing software.

A variety of filters on the Instagram app allow you to quickly alter the look and feel of your photos with just the touch of a button.

For video, simply touch the video camera icon to the right of the camera. A large red button will appear to let you know you are in video mode. Videos can be no longer than fifteen seconds. Video is recorded as long as your finger is held on the red button, up to a maximum of fifteen seconds. You can make edits or jump cuts by taking your finger off the button, focusing on another subject, and recording again on something else. Even crude stop-motion and other animation can be achieved by making many quick cuts. Add filters, adjust the color, get creative, and see what you can do!

## Sharing

After you have your photo or video just the way you want it, it's now time to share it with friends and family. Simply click the Next button at the top right of the screen. You will then have the option to add a caption to describe your picture or video. You can also "tag," or identify, other Instagram friends in your picture. This will send them a notification that they have been tagged.

Depending on the phone you use, you will see sharing choices such as Facebook, Flickr, Twitter, and Tumblr. You will need to have existing accounts to share content directly to these sites. You can also click the e-mail choice to e-mail the photo. It is also possible just to click the Share icon at the bottom of the screen. If no other choices are made, the photo will be shared to all your Instagram contacts and appear on their feeds.

# Chapter 2

# Other Photo and Video Apps

**B**efore mobile photo sharing, if you wanted to share pictures with friends and family you'd have to buy film, shoot the twenty-four to thirty-six shots, drop the rolls off to be developed into prints, return to pick them up, and then finally put them in an album and show them to people. Today, all that has changed and most people do not even bother making prints from their pictures. If they do make prints, oftentimes this can be easily accomplished at home with a printer. Sharing photos with friends and family, can now be done instantly via mobile devices and photo apps. They can be shared to your Instagram feed or other sites, with many people viewing the photos at once.

While Instagram may be the best-known mobile photo-sharing app, there are many others. If you decide you want to move beyond Instagram or use another photo-sharing app entirely, you might feel frustrated because there are just so many of them to choose from. These apps offer features and ways of sharing on different apps that offer the user more choices and open up many exciting creative possibilities. Here are some of the other photo apps you might find useful for downloading and using.

## Snapchat

Snapchat is a very different photo-sharing app from Instagram. After Snapchat has been downloaded, you will need to take many of the same steps you did when creating an Instagram account. Your e-mail, a username, and a password will all be required to get going. Once up and running, the app will give you the ability to share photos with friends or a group of friends, with one major difference: the images shared are not permanently stored. When you send a picture to a friend with Snapchat, you choose how long the recipient can see the picture before it disappears from the screen forever. The most common time limit is between one and ten seconds. A friend receiving a photo of yours that you have given a

Snapchat is a photo-sharing app in which the photos sent between users disappear after a short amount of time.

ten-second time limit will be able to see the picture on his mobile device for ten seconds. After that, POOF! The picture disappears from his phone and is erased from Snapchat servers.

Why would anyone want an app that does not save the images taken with it? Well, kids like secrets. While you don't mind sharing many pictures you take with others, you might want to share some only with a single family member or close friend. Pictures in Snapchat can be drawn on with a virtual stylus before they are sent. Writing a short message or creatively coloring and cartooning over pictures in wacky and creative ways may be fun, but it might not be something you want everyone to see. The fleeting existence of the picture taken with Snapchat is the very point of the app, and it is very popular with teens between the ages of thirteen and eighteen. The app is not intended for use by kids under the age of thirteen. And be aware that, although your photo disappears, it may not be gone for good. Users have found ways around this limitation, so exercise extreme caution when using Snapchat.

## Memoir

Each time you might think all the possible features that can be invented for mobile photo-sharing apps have been thought of, up pops another app that does something different in a new and creative way. Memoir is a photo-sharing and retrieval app for all the photos you have taken with other apps. Once you create your account, you will need to give Memoir permission to access the various accounts you use to share photos, such as Instagram and Facebook. Memoir then takes all those photos and organizes them into a private personal memoir only for you.

This is a new way to access and see the many photos you have taken and stored on various services. For example, you can ask Memoir to show you photos from this date last year. It will retrieve photos, if you posted any, on the same date but last year or several years back. It's a great way to see not just recent images, but also old images that spark memories. Enter your birth date and see all of your birthday photos from previous years.

Many apps that you will use on your phone have sites on the Internet that allow you to view the images on your computer as well.

Once created, you can choose to share your personal memoir with other Memoir users. This is the social aspect of this app. Once connected with another user, you can see various events that you may have both been present at and see pictures taken by other users that you do not have stored in your social networks. This app is very personal and allows close friends and family to share photos and see a mixture of different people's photos that may have all been taken at the same event in the past. Taking new pictures in the app is also possible.

File   Edit   View   Favorites   Tools   Help

APPS, APPS EVERYWHERE, BUT WHICH ONE TO CHOOSE?

## APPS, APPS EVERYWHERE, BUT WHICH ONE TO CHOOSE?

There are so many apps available and more being created every day! Which one to choose can often be confusing and complex. A good rule of thumb is to use what your friends already use. This way, you will be able to communicate and share with more people. Even the best photo-sharing app is of little use if no one you know is using it.

## Vine

Vine is for taking, posting, and viewing short looping videos. The app is set up very much like Instagram but has no option for still photography. Vine videos can be about seven seconds in length. There is no Record button in Vine. To take a video, you simply put your finger on the screen and hold it there till the green progress bar scrolls to the end. At any point during your recording, you can pause recording and restart by applying your finger back on the pad. Many interesting and creative, and often funny, looping videos can be made this way.

Completed videos can be shared with Vine contacts or to Twitter or Facebook. The option to copy the Vine link for a specific video is available, so the user can e-mail or post the video anywhere else on the web beyond the few sites offered in the app.

As with all other apps, getting parental permission to use Vine is a must. When you enter the app, you are provided a feed of publicly shared videos from other Vine users, whether you know them or not. This may be a concern for some parents, so be sure you are aware of your personal rules and limitations.

Vine is a video-sharing app that takes short videos that can be posted on a Vine feed or shared to social media sites.

# Mobli

Mobli is a photo and video app with editing tools built in. Filters and photo effects can also be applied to pictures. The app has hashtag suggestions and built-in direct-messaging features. Unlike many other video apps, Mobli has no limit on the length of videos you can take.

While Mobli has many desirable features, it does not have as many users as Instagram. For this reason, Mobli has a special feature that lets you move photos into other apps to share them with a wider audience.

# Online Storage

Uploading photos to social media websites such as Twitter, Google+, or Facebook is not the only option for sharing photos. Photo-storage sites are also available as places to put photos online and even share them. Flickr, Snapfish, Shutterfly, and Photobucket are just a few of the more popular photo-storage sites. They each have mobile apps with built-in camera features for posting pictures. Friends can be invited to view your albums.

Take the time to explore and investigate which app or site will suit your needs. A site such as Flickr, for instance, is best for someone who shoots and uploads lots of pictures to be shared with the online photo community. Within Flickr there are hundreds of specialized groups for every type and style of photo you can imagine. Many professional photographers use Flickr to share their work. You don't need to upload to explore, and you don't need a mobile device to post photos there. Photo-storage sites such as Flickr can be a great option for people who don't have a cell phone or tablet with a built-in camera.

# MYTHS & FACTS

**MYTH** I need a smartphone to share digital photos with my friends online.

**FACT** You can easily share digital photos online from your home computer.

**MYTH** Most photo-sharing apps and editing apps cost money.

**FACT** Many popular photo-sharing apps and editing apps are free to download.

**MYTH** Everyone is using social networks.

**FACT** Many younger kids are not allowed or are restricted in their use of cell phones and the Internet.

# Chapter 3

# Being Responsible and Staying Safe

**U**nless you are an adult, it's very likely that you are not the one paying for the mobile phone and mobile photo-sharing services you are currently using. While many apps are free, they still require a paid Wi-Fi or data plan, a cell phone that comes with a monthly bill, and a home computer that all cost your parent or guardian money.

When an app is free, you should consider everything that does cost money before that app can be downloaded and used. Also, consider that you are allowed to use these services because you have been given permission to do so from an adult. The fact that you are using a mobile device shows that an adult has placed a certain amount of trust in you that you will use the device appropriately.

## A Privilege, Not a Right

There are many young adults, and even many adults, who do not want or cannot afford to have mobile phones themselves. Always respect your parents' decisions and follow their judgment about using your mobile device. If

Children and teens must rely on their parents' permission before using photo- and video-sharing apps.

you are not allowed to have a mobile phone while others around you are, take heart and understand that parents do change their minds about technology use as children get older.

Although they have become an important part of our world, keep in mind that cell phones are still a relatively new gadget. Only a few short years ago, no mobile technologies were readily available. Generally considered the first smartphone, the first generation of the iPhone was released on June 29, 2007. Phones back in the 1970s were wired to the wall and did not even have buttons! You had to dial the numbers one by one on a rotary

File    Edit    View    Favorites    Tools    Help

— ☐ X

BEYOND YOUR SOCIAL CIRCLE... IMPACT ON THE WORLD

## BEYOND YOUR SOCIAL CIRCLE... IMPACT ON THE WORLD

In early 2011, several Middle Eastern and North African countries underwent a political and social upheaval, known as the Arab Spring. Led largely by young people, photos and videos of antigovernment protests were captured on mobile devices and uploaded to social networking sites. News of these events spread faster than any other current events or news stories in history. People were able to gather in city squares at a moment's notice, and media outlets caught on to the stories instantly. Some of the protests eventually led to the unseating of dictators and the changing of oppressive policies that had been in place for generations. Instagram, Twitter, Facebook, and other sites played an important role in these government and civil rights struggles. While photo and video apps are fun and useful for communicating, remember that the tool can also impact your world.

ring. So remember that even the technologies you so desperately wish you had today will soon be replaced by something new.

No matter what the specifics of your mobile phone situation are, always be sure to discuss the rules your parents or guardians have set for you. Also, be aware that most mobile phone plans have data plans that allow for only a certain amount of communication or data to be used when you are out and about and not connected to a Wi-Fi network.

When uploading and downloading photos and videos on your mobile device while out and about, you will be accessing cellular communications networks. Photos and videos sent from your mobile device are often considered data. Find out what the limits are for the plan being used by your family. Talk with your parents about what limits they expect from you as far as calls, Internet use, texting, and mobile photo sharing. Listen and respect whatever house rules are laid down. Breaking these rules may cost your parents unexpected extra charges on their cell phone bill.

## Digital Footprint

Everything that a person posts to the Internet contributes to what is commonly called a digital footprint. This is a sort of cyber version of yourself that can be searched, stumbled upon, and seen by others. Just because you share something with a friend and you consider the communication completely private, you should be aware that this might not always be the case.

Remember that photos you snap and share can be seen by many other people, including friends and schoolmates.

Any photo or video you share with another person or post to the Internet can and may take on a life of its own. Your friends may choose to share your image with others or at least show it to others. Your friends' mobile phones will likely be monitored by their parents. Mobile phones can also be lost and then found by strangers. Despite all your careful efforts with the privacy and security settings on your cell phone, your friends may not be as careful.

What can one do in the face of such uncertainty? The first thing is never to share something you would not be comfortable with anyone or everyone seeing. Think first before you post! Always treat your friends' photos the same way you'd want them to treat yours.

Also, do not think of apps such as Snapchat as an excuse to send a photo of anything you wish. Some teens may think that because the photos disappear, their friend will be the only one to see them. That may be true, but what if someone else picks up your friend's phone, such as your friend's sibling or parent? That may likely mean that person saw the photo that was intended for your friend, and your friend may never have seen it at all. Even when you are in the middle of a texting conversation with a friend, distractions can happen quickly. You can't be sure if or when your friend is called away. Remember, send only images that you wouldn't mind others seeing.

## Cyberbullying

A bully is someone who bothers or harasses another person either with words or physical force. It is important to be aware that bullying can happen online and via mobile photo-sharing apps. When someone is bullied online, it is often referred to as cyberbullying. Cyberbullying on mobile photo-sharing apps can occur in the form of inappropriate pictures, harmful or hurtful comments, or even harassing videos. With screen names to hide behind, cyberbullies may find that bullying through photo-sharing apps is even easier than face-to-face bullying.

Never post images or videos that can be hurtful to someone else. Participating in these digital activities is considered cyberbullying.

If someone, even a friend, is behaving in a way that makes you uncomfortable or you suspect is inappropriate, always tell an adult and share what you have observed. Never keep cyberbullying to yourself.

## Being a Good Friend

Everyone knows that life is easier and more enjoyable with good friends to help and support you. The same goes for the online world. Remember to think of your friends when you are taking photos at an event. You may wish to remember or share a certain moment, but your friend may feel otherwise. Don't take pictures if someone in the photo objects to the idea. Think about that person's feelings and her reasons for not wanting you to take or share the photograph. You don't have to agree with the person, but you should certainly respect the person's ideas and wishes.

It may be "your" photo because you snapped it with your phone, but people who see it online will be thinking of the friends they see in it, not the person who took it. Similarly, if someone asks you to delete a picture after it is posted, be considerate to that person as well. Remember that once a photo is posted on the Internet, the number of people who are likely to see it takes off like a rocket. Videos with sound can be damaging if friends are caught saying something unflattering about another classmate, teacher, or family member. Watch what you say, and look out for your friends in the online world.

# TEN GREAT QUESTIONS

## TO ASK A TECHNOLOGY TEACHER

1   What should I do if my friend is being bullied on social media but doesn't want help?

2   Why don't teachers let us use cell phones at school?

3   What can I do if my friends are using photo-sharing apps that my parents won't let me download?

4   What should I do if someone posted a picture of me that I don't want others to see?

5   What should I do if I get inappropriate photos from acquaintances?

6   I keep getting notifications to update my apps. Should I always update?

7   How can I get a refund if I downloaded a photo-editing app that costs money, but I don't want it?

8   How do I back up my photos when my phone becomes full and has no more space?

9   How do I protect my photos if I lose my phone?

10   How can I access my photos if I lose my phone?

# Chapter 4

# Great Tips for Using Photo and Video Apps

**A**side from just snapping and sharing photos and videos with your friends, mobile photo- and video-sharing apps offer you a fantastic creative tool right in the palm of your hand. After all, you see the world differently from your friends. There are countless creative ways to use photo and video apps for yourself, your family and friends, and even for your school projects. But before you plan your projects, here are some tips for taking the best photos possible.

## Tips for Great Pics

The cameras built into today's cellular devices make it easy to take good photos. They have autofocus, and they even have automatic settings that allow the user to just snap the photo and not worry about lighting or exposure times. These are great features that help the user get quick, clear pictures on the go. However, there are still ways to control the subject and the camera to make your pictures come out even better than a quick snapshot.

## Keep Still

One common photo problem is blurry pictures. This can happen because either the photographer or the subject is moving. Cameras have settings that help eliminate motion blur, but mobile phones are not professional cameras. Keeping still while you are taking a photo and asking your subject to keep still is the simplest and most effective trick for getting consistently sharp, focused photos from a mobile phone or tablet camera.

Different framing and composition techniques can give each photographer a different result, even of an iconic landmark such as the Empire State Building.

## Frame Your Shot

Before you snap a picture, decide exactly where to point the camera. This may sound like an obvious piece of advice, but it can go a long way toward getting great photos. A shot might have your friends in the frame from head to toe, with a lot of their surroundings also visible. Shots like this can be interesting if the location is also interesting. If, however, the location is not entirely important, then moving in closer and cropping out people's lower bodies in favor of head shots can be a lot more appealing. If the lighting around you is good, remember to turn off the flash because it can overexpose pictures. Experiment with how you crop your photos.

## Experiment

Try taking a few shots of the same subject from far, medium, and close distances until you find the best way to observe and see your subject matter. While it's true that you can always crop photos later once you put them on your computer, think about how much easier it would be if you framed the photo well in the first place.

Subjects may look good with several different treatments. For example, flowers in a pot on a deck with your yard in the background will look one way. Taking a close-up of the flowers with the sky behind them will have a different look and feel. There are infinite ways to shoot a single subject. If you're not sure how you want the picture to look, try a little experimentation. You can always delete the ones you do not like when you are going through them.

# Think About the Presentation

After taking the shots you want, it's time to present them in an appealing way. One creative way to present photos is by putting together a slide show. Slide show presentations can make great gifts, and they can be fun ways to remember events or friendships. Android phones and iPhones both offer

Photos that were not composed perfectly when taken can be adjusted within apps such as Instagram before sharing.

the feature that allows for taking specific pictures and creating albums. From there, you can easily select the slide show display option. Aside from showing photos on your mobile device, you might be able to display slide shows on your home TV. Apple TV allows content from iPhones and iPads to be streamed to a TV.

Another fun way to present photos is with a photo collage. You may have seen photo collages show up in your Instagram feed. They are several photos arranged, or collaged, together within the border of a single picture. Instagram does not have the feature available within the app, but there are other apps that you can download that allow you to get creative and group a few shots together.

Diptic, Pic Stitch, Photo Grid, and PhotoShake! are all great apps for choosing from a few photos and grouping them together. Think of a basketball game you attended with friends at which you took some shots. You may have photographed someone making a basket in the game, friends cheering, and a shot of a basketball on the ground. All three photos can be collaged into one frame with either app. Then you can share this photo via Instagram or many of the other photo-sharing apps available.

Getting creative like this can add more personality to your photos. After you shoot for a while, you will develop a taste for the kinds of pictures you like to take and how you enjoy presenting them. You may have some friends who love using collages, while others prefer to use filters or post videos. Developing a style can become part of your digital footprint. Collage apps, filters, color adjustments, framing, and your choice of subject matter all add up to making your pictures unique and part of your personal style.

## Photos and Videos as Educational Tools

If you get a little creative, photo and video apps can have a great place in the classroom. Multimedia reports can be made with the help of your favorite apps, combining your creative knowledge, technical skills, and schoolwork. For example, with permission from your teacher, you might take videos or photos on a class trip and make a report of the event afterward. When

The photos you take and share with photo apps can be used for educational purposes during school reports and presentations.

doing a research project, you can use video interviews or include short snippets of footage recorded from documentaries. With editing programs, you can put together credits and divide the video into sections. Your video can then be presented online or to the whole class over a multimedia hookup in your classroom.

A slide show is a good way to present photos during an oral presentation. Instead of using presentation software such as PowerPoint, try taking photos with your mobile device and displaying a slide show from your phone or tablet onto a larger screen. Adding music may also be an option,

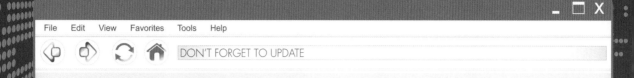

File    Edit    View    Favorites    Tools    Help

DON'T FORGET TO UPDATE

## DON'T FORGET TO UPDATE

Regardless of the devices that come out in the future, consumers must continue to keep current on the apps and devices that they already use. While the basics of photography and framing a great picture remain the same, the apps and devices will be constantly changing. Updates are designed to make using apps easier and more streamlined. Annoying problems or bugs that you encounter with some apps may be fixed with new software updates. Over time, updates also help apps work more smoothly with Internet browser updates. Each time you update, remember to become familiar with any new features before using the app.

depending on the app you choose for presenting the photos. Using technology in a creative and productive way can help make parents and teachers see the positive potential of digital devices. Instead of seeing cell phones as a distraction for students, they may see the positive impact the technology can have on learning.

## What the Future Holds

If you could look into a crystal ball and see what the future of mobile devices holds, what would you see? Many experts believe that wearable gadgets such as smartwatches and Google Glass will be the wave of the future.

Google Glass is a hands-free wearable mobile device developed by the Internet giant Google. It is a computer that sits on your head, just as eyeglasses do. A tiny optical display sits above the field of view of the user's

The cutting edge of wearable mobile photo technology is Google Glass. Users can photograph their surroundings or access the Internet with a variety of installed apps.

right eye. The unit also includes the ability to take photos and video, connect to the Internet, and even make and receive phone calls when tethered to a mobile phone.

With each new innovative digital device comes new challenges as far as safety, etiquette, and especially privacy. Concerns about privacy have been raised with Google Glass because of its ability to snap photos and videos discreetly.

Staying flexible, creative, and curious about mobile technology can keep you ready for the changes that lie ahead in the exciting world of photo and video apps.

# GLOSSARY

**application** A software program that runs on a computer to achieve a specific purpose for the user.

**collage** A grouping of photos or art arranged together, often in a pleasing way.

**composition** The deliberately selective and creative way a photo is framed.

**cyberbully** A person who posts mean-spirited messages through the Internet about a person to harass him or her.

**data plan** An agreement that determines the specific cost for the amount of data a person's cell phone can upload and download within a predetermined amount of time.

**digital footprint** Digital information about you that has been posted or stored on the Internet.

**exposure** The amount of time a camera's shutter remains open to the image being taken.

**film** A light-sensitive strip of plastic or other material used to record pictures on before the invention of digital cameras.

**filter** A tool within a photo app for manipulating the way an image looks.

**jump cut** An edit in video that switches between subjects.

**selective focus** When only part of an entire photo is in focus.

**selfie** A portrait taken of oneself, usually with a mobile phone.

**smartphone** A portable phone with a computer incorporated into it, giving it the ability to take pictures and video, and run multiple applications.

**social media** Photos, videos, texts, and other content created to be shared with others on the web or via mobile devices.

**stylus** A pen-like implement often used to write or draw on touchscreen computers.

**Wi-Fi** A wireless connection that allows mobile devices and computers to connect to the Internet.

# FOR MORE INFORMATION

Canadian Centre for Child Protection
615 Academy Road
Winnipeg, MB R3N 0E7
Canada
(204) 945-5735
Website: https://www.protectchildren.ca
The Canadian Centre for Child Protection is a charitable organization that
    works to protect children, including those involved in cyberbullying.

High Tech Kids
111 3rd Avenue South, Suite 145
Minneapolis, MN 55401
(612) 781-2203
Website: http://www.hightechkids.org
High Tech Kids is a Minnesota-based organization that caters to students
    interested in science, engineering, and technology programs.

Kids with Cameras
122 Main Street
Salt Lake City, UT 84101
(801) 746-7000
Website: http://www.kids-with-cameras.org
Kids with Cameras is a nonprofit organization that teaches photography to
    children in struggling communities around the world.

MediaSmarts: Canada's Centre for Digital and Media Literacy
950 Gladstone Avenue, Suite 120
Ottawa, ON K1Y 3E6
Canada

(613) 224-7721
Website: http://mediasmarts.ca
MediaSmarts is an organization dedicated to digital and media literacy for
 teens, including making wise decisions online.

Technology Student Association (TSA)
1914 Association Drive
Reston, VA 20191-1540
(703) 860-9000
Website: http://www.tsaweb.org
The TSA is an organization of middle and high school students who aspire to
 learn more about science and technology.

Young Photographer's Alliance
9965 Leroy Pavilion Road
Pavilion, NY 14525
(585) 768-7880
Website: http://www.youngphotographersalliance.org
The Young Photographer's Alliance is a nonprofit organization that provides
 mentoring, scholarships, and educational lectures to young people inter-
 ested in photography.

## Websites

Because of the changing nature of Internet links, Rosen Publishing has developed
an online list of websites related to the subject of this book. This site is updated
regularly. Please use this link to access the list:

http://www.rosenlinks.com/DIL/Inst

# FOR FURTHER READING

Ang, Tom. *How to Photograph Absolutely Everything: Successful Pictures from Your Digital Camera*. New York, NY: DK Publishing, 2009.

Binder, Jenni. *The Kids' Guide to Digital Photography: How to Shoot, Save, Play with & Print Your Digital Photos*. New York, NY: Sterling Press, 2011.

Chapman, Emma, and Elsie Larson. *A Beautiful Mess Photo Idea Book: 95 Inspiring Ideas for Photographing Your Friends, Your World, and Yourself*. New York, NY: Potter Style, 2013.

Gardener, Howard, and Katie Davis. *The App Generation: How Today's Youth Navigate Identity, Intimacy, and Imagination in a Digital World*. New Haven, CT: Yale University Press, 2013.

Graham, Jefferson. *Video Nation: A DIY Guide to Planning, Shooting, and Sharing Great Video from USA Today's Talking Tech Host*. San Francisco, CA: Peachpit Press, 2012.

Gupta, Amit, and Kelly Jensen. *Photojojo!: Insanely Great Photo Projects and DIY Ideas*. New York, NY: Potter Craft, 2009.

Harbour, Sarita. *Instagram: How a Photo-Sharing App Achieved a $1 Billion Facebook Buyout in 18 Months*. Seattle, WA: Amazon Digital Services, 2012.

Hoffman, Allan. *Create Great iPhone Photos: Apps, Tips, Tricks, and Effects*. San Francisco, CA: No Starch Press, 2011.

Holmberg, Martina. *Sixty Tips for Creative iPhone Photography*. Santa Barbara, CA: Rocky Nook, 2012.

Keller, Steven. *iPhone Photography Tips and Tricks: How to Take Great Pictures with Your iPhone Camera and Apps*. Seattle, WA: Amazon Digital Services, 2012.

Macarthy, Andrew. *100 Instagram Tips, Tricks and Secrets: Take Photos Like a Pro, Get More Followers, and Discover the Best Instagram Apps*. Seattle, WA: Amazon Digital Services, 2012.

Marcolina, Dan. *iPhone Obsessed: Photo Editing Experiments with Apps.*
    San Francisco, CA: Peachpit Press, 2011.
Miotke, Jim. *Better Photo Basics: The Absolute Beginner's Guide to Taking
    Photos Like a Pro.* New York, NY: Amphoto Books, 2010.
Sonheim, Carla, and Steve Sonheim. *Creative Photography Lab: 52 Fun
    Exercises for Developing Self-Expression with Your Camera.*
    Minneapolis, MN: Quarry Books, 2013.
Watson-Novacek, Deborah. *Instagram for Beginners.* Seattle, WA: The
    Escape Project, 2012.

# BIBLIOGRAPHY

Agence France-Presse. "About 800 Billion Photographs Will Be Taken in 2014—Including a Lot of Selfies." BusinessInsider.com, December 24, 2013. Retrieved January 2, 2014 (http://www.businessinsider.com/selfies-and-2013-2013-12).

Berkman, Fran. "Revolution in Egypt Captured Through Eye of a Camera." Mashable.com, August 22, 2013. Retrieved January 4, 2014 (http://mashable.com/2013/08/22/egypt-revolution-photographer).

Brumfield, Ben. "Selfie Named Word of the Year for 2013." CNN.com, November 20, 2013. Retrieved January 10, 2014 (http://www.cnn.com/2013/11/19/living/selfie-word-of-the-year).

Diallo, Amadou. "Five Quick Tips for Better Instagram Photos." Forbes.com, August 31, 2013. Retrieved January 10, 2014 (http://www.forbes.com/sites/amadoudiallo/2013/08/31/five-quick-tips-for-better-instagram-photos).

Get the Facts. "Digital Footprint." Cybersmart.gov. Retrieved January 3, 2014 (http://www.cybersmart.gov.au/Kids/Get%20the%20facts/Digital%20footprint.aspx).

Kay, Mary. "How to Prevent Mobile Phone Cyberbullying—Know the Warning Signs and What to Do." YourSphere.com, May 1, 2013. Retrieved January 14, 2014 (http://internet-safety.yoursphere.com/2013/05/how-to-prevent-mobile-phone-cyberbullying-learn-the-warning-signs-and-what-to-do).

Keenan, Cody. "A Day in the Life: Inside the State of the Union with Cody Keenan." Whitehouse.gov, January 22, 2014. Retrieved January 22, 2014 (http://m.whitehouse.gov/blog/2014/01/22/day-life-inside-state-union-cody-keenan?utm_source=email&utm_medium=email&utm_content=email286-text1&utm_campaign=sotu).

Lyons, Patrick J. "Polaroid Abandons Instant Photography." TheLede.com, February 8, 2008. Retrieved January 2, 2014 (http://thelede .blogs.nytimes.com/2008/02/08/polaroid-abandons-instant -photography/?_r=0).

Photo Sharing Apps. "Photo Sharing." Appadvice.com. Retrieved January 2, 2014 (http://appadvice.com/applists/show/photo-sharing-apps).

Silver, Leigh. "The Polaroid Years' Book Explores the Retro Camera's Influence on Photography." HuffingtonPost.com, June 3, 2013. Retrieved January 2, 2014 (http://www.huffingtonpost.com/2013/06/03/the -polaroid-years-instant-photography-and-experimentation-mary-kay -lombino-book_n_3327903.html).

Tumbokon, Karen. "Top 10 Best Photo-Sharing Apps for Your Android Device or iPhone." Heavy.com, August 25, 2013. Retrieved December 14, 2013 (http://www.heavy.com/tech/2013/08/top-best -photo-sharing-apps-for-android-ios-iphone-2013/).

Wortham, Jenna. "Instagram Direct Takes Photo-Sharing Private." *New York Times*, December 12, 2013. Retrieved December 12, 2013 (http:// bits.blogs.nytimes.com/2013/12/12/instagram-introduces-private -messaging/?_php=true&_type=blogs&ref=business&_r=1&gwh=25FF D00A8768B41B1E2A2799F4EBF8C6&gwt=pay).

# INDEX

## About the Author

Seen more frequently behind a camera than in front of it, Adam Furgang has been snapping photos for more than thirty years. He attended the High School of Art and Design, the University of the Arts, and has worked as a graphic designer, web designer, fine artist, freelance photographer, and finally…a writer. Furgang finds ways to integrate his love for photography into everything he does and always has his mobile phone with him to capture the tiny details of life. He is currently taking his love for mobile gadget photography to the extreme in the Google Glass Explorer program, testing out the latest model of Google Glass and its photo and video capabilities. His photographic influences include Diane Arbus, Man Ray, Andy Warhol, and Henri Cartier-Bresson. He lives in upstate New York with his favorite photo subjects—his wife and two sons.

## Photo Credits